The Wallace Collection
GUIDE

The Trustees of the Wallace Collection, Manchester Square,
London W1M 6BN
1996

ISBN 0 900785 60 8

Contents

PREFACE

The Wallace Collection is continually changing. Since our last guide book, we have refurbished the Entrance Hall, the Inner Hall, the Grand Staircase, Gallery 5 (Sir Richard Wallace's Front State Room) and, more recently, Gallery 4. We are striving to improve our gallery lighting and labelling, to offer new scholarly catalogues (*The Wallace Collection Catalogue of Furniture* by Peter Hughes in 1996) and to continue our new programme of conservation first aid, particularly for the furniture. As these changes continue, no guide book can be perfect; I apologize if you find unexpected minor alterations in the galleries contrary to the information contained here.

Manchester Square is also changing and since January 1996 we have had a new neighbour, the printing company Watmoughs (Holdings) PLC. They have offered immediate support to the Wallace Collection by generously printing this guide book for us free of charge. I am especially grateful to Watmoughs' Executive Chairman, Mr Patrick Walker, for his enthusiastic sponsorship which I hope will bring pleasure to all who read this book. I am also grateful to Alliance Paper Group PLC for so kindly supplying the paper for this edition at a reduced price. Finally I want to thank my curatorial colleagues Stephen Duffy, Robert Wenley and David Edge, whose careful compilation of this comprehensive guide will enable you to feel more at home with the Wallace Collection and its collectors.

You may wonder what plans we have for our future since the year 2000 will be our centenary as a national museum. We have very exciting plans for the basement and courtyard of Hertford House. In the basement we need to create new galleries for temporary exhibitions, the reserve collection, light-sensitive materials and conservation projects, materials and techniques. We also plan a lecture theatre, schools room and seminar room, and a drop-in library with easy access to our historic sales catalogues and archives. Then, following visitors' wishes shown in surveys, we plan to float a glass roof over the courtyard to create a Sculpture Garden with a café which will also be available for hire in the evenings. All of this will unobtrusively underpin and strengthen the integrity and special qualities of the galleries, and will offer the visitor a more extensive and enjoyable time in the Wallace Collection.

Finally, as you leave the Collection, you might like to mark your visit in two ways. Firstly, we provide a Visitors' Book in the Hall for you to make comments and suggestions and we always welcome your views. Secondly, if you have enjoyed your visit, you might like to contribute to the donations boxes in the Outer Hall. In both cases you would be assisting us in our efforts to care for this unique national collection. Thank you.

Rosalind Savill
Director

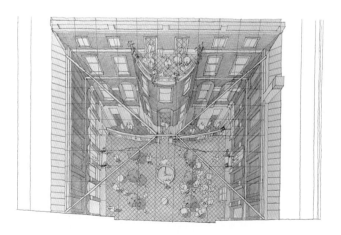

Aerial view of the proposed new Courtyard Sculpture Garden

Ground floor

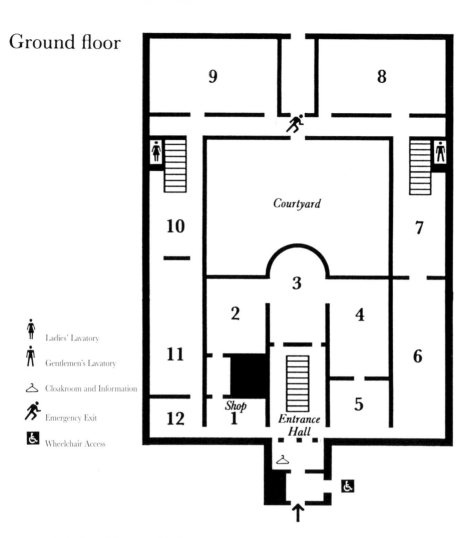

Ladies' Lavatory

Gentlemen's Lavatory

Cloakroom and Information

Emergency Exit

Wheelchair Access

1 & Corridor	SHOP
2-4	French 18th-century furniture and paintings (Sèvres porcelain in Gallery 4)
5	English portraits and French 18th-century furniture
6, 7 & Corridor	Medieval, Renaissance and Baroque works of art
8-11	Arms and armour (Orientalist paintings in Gallery 11)
12	English and French paintings of the 1820s and 1830s

First floor

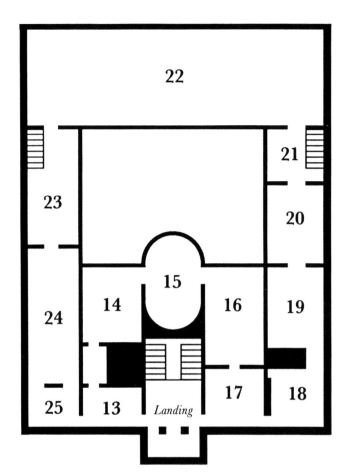

Introduction

The Wallace Collection was bequeathed to the nation in February 1897 by Lady Wallace. She was the widow of Sir Richard Wallace, a notable collector of works of art and also, as the illegitimate son of the 4th Marquess of Hertford, the inheritor of one of the greatest of all private collections.

By the terms of Lady Wallace's bequest the Collection is named The Wallace Collection and it remains together 'unmixed with other objects of art'. Because nothing may therefore be loaned or added it enshrines an Anglo-French nineteenth-century taste. Among its many treasures are one of the finest collections of French eighteenth-century pictures, porcelain and furniture outside Paris, a remarkable display of seventeenth-century paintings and a superb armoury.

The Wallace Collection is kept at Hertford House, which had been the principal London residence of the Marquesses of Hertford and was later owned by Sir Richard Wallace. It opened to the public as a national museum in June 1900.

The Founders

The 1st Marquess of Hertford

Francis Seymour-Conway (1719-94). Descended from the Edward Seymour who became Lord Protector of England in 1547 and was the brother of Queen Jane Seymour. A loyal Tory courtier, he was Ambassador in Paris (1762-5), Lord Lieutenant of Ireland (1765-6) and Lord Chamberlain (1766-82). His family's property included Ragley Hall in Warwickshire (still the country seat of the Marquesses of Hertford), Conway Castle, Sudbourne Hall in Suffolk and extensive estates in Ireland. He bought six of the Canalettos now in the Collection.

The 2nd Marquess of Hertford

Francis Ingram Seymour-Conway (1743-1822), son of the 1st Marquess. Like his father a loyal Tory, he was Lord of the Treasury (1774-82), Ambassador to Berlin and Vienna (1793-94) and Lord Chamberlain (1812-21). This last appointment was facilitated by the considerable influence

Hertford House

9

that his wife gained over the Prince of Wales, later George IV. In 1797 he acquired the lease of Manchester House (now Hertford House). He bought some notable English portraits, including Reynolds's *Nelly O'Brien*, and was given Gainsborough's *'Perdita' Robinson* by the Prince of Wales. Some pieces of Sèvres porcelain now in the Collection were also acquired by him.

The 3rd Marquess of Hertford

The 3rd Marquess of Hertford, *c.* 1825

Francis Charles Seymour-Conway (1777-1842), son of the 2nd Marquess. He was Vice-Chamberlain in the Royal Household (1812-21). In 1798 he married Maria Fagnani, the illegitimate daughter of the Marchesa Fagnani. She greatly increased the family fortunes through substantial bequests from the 4th Duke of Queensberry ('Old Q') and his associate George Selwyn who both believed that they were her father. The future 4th Marquess was born of this marriage in 1800, but when the 3rd Marquess and Maria visited Paris in 1802 they became estranged and thereafter led separate lives. She remained in Paris where in 1805 she gave birth to a second son, the future Lord Henry Seymour (whose father was probably Count Casimir de Montrond), while the 3rd Marquess established splendid residences in London at Dorchester House (on the site of the present Dorchester Hotel) and at St Dunstan's Villa in Regent's Park (demolished in 1937). His later life was devoted largely to dissipation and foreign travel to the extent that both Thackeray (Lord Steyne in *Vanity Fair*) and Disraeli (Lord Monmouth in *Coningsby*) chose him as the model for sinister characters.

The 3rd Marquess was a considerable connoisseur. He bought seventeenth-century Dutch cabinet pictures (including Netscher's *Lacemaker* and the Rembrandtesque *Good Samaritan* and *Landscape with a Coach*), French furniture, gilt bronzes and Sèvres porcelain. He also acted as a saleroom agent for the Prince of Wales, for whom he bought outstanding Dutch pictures which remain in the Royal Collection. Both men were attracted by the luxury and refinement of eighteenth-century French art and, like other English collectors, profited from the dissolution of many Continental collections during the French Revolution and the Napoleonic wars.

The 4th Marquess of Hertford

The 4th Marquess of Hertford, *c.* 1855

Richard Seymour-Conway (1800-70), son of the 3rd Marquess, was brought up in Paris by his mother and came to England in 1816. He was briefly an M.P. (1819-26) and a cavalry officer. In 1829 he visited Constantinople. By 1835, when he purchased the château of Bagatelle in the Bois de Boulogne, he had determined to forgo any public duties and to settle in Paris. He then lived mostly in a large apartment at no.2 rue Laffitte (near his mother, her second son, Lord Henry Seymour, and his own illegitimate son Richard Jackson).

The 4th Marquess never married. Witty and intelligent as well as one of the richest men in Europe, he sometimes ventured into Parisian society and became friendly with Napoleon III. But there was a neurotic side to his personality and he preferred a reclusive life. He 'would not even have drawn back his curtain to see a revolution go past in the street' wrote one contemporary, Charles Yriarte. In 1845 he visited the Irish estates from which he derived much of his income. After a stay of five weeks, he went back to Paris, resolving never to return.

The last thirty years of the 4th Marquess's life were devoted to collecting works of art. He bought Dutch paintings (including Rembrandt's *Titus* and Hals's *The Laughing Cavalier*), many superb old masters (including masterpieces by Poussin, van Dyck, Velázquez and Rubens) and most of the early nineteenth-century French and English paintings now at Hertford House. Like his father, he was attracted by the superb craftsmanship of the *ancien régime*, but he acquired a wider range of objects and on a far larger scale. He bought pictures by Watteau, Greuze, Boucher and Fragonard; many fine pieces of Sèvres porcelain; furniture by the greatest French cabinet-makers of the eighteenth century such as Gaudreaus and Riesener, as well as miniatures, gold boxes, tapestries and sculpture. For most of his collecting life the art of the *ancien régime* had still not fully recovered from its disparagement during the French Revolution and the First Empire. In his last decade he acquired the important collection of Oriental arms and armour.

He usually bought at auction through agents, and from the letters to his main London agent, Samuel Mawson, we know something of his motivations as a collector. His taste tended towards the pleasing and the sensuous (hence his liking for the paintings of Murillo with their 'rich,

11

mellow quality') and he attached great importance to good condition and a known (particularly royal) provenance. He apparently did not visit England after 1855 and perhaps never saw some of his finest purchases, such as *The Rainbow Landscape* by Rubens, which were sent directly from the London salerooms to Hertford House.

He died at Bagatelle in August 1870 as the Prussian army advanced on Paris, bringing the Second Empire to an end. He bequeathed his unentailed property, including his great collection, to his illegitimate son, Richard Wallace. The Marquisate was inherited by a second cousin.

Sir Richard Wallace, 1888

Sir Richard Wallace

Richard Jackson (1818-90), the illegitimate son of the 4th Marquess of Hertford and Mrs Agnes Jackson, was raised in Paris by his grandmother from the age of six. The 4th Marquess never acknowledged his paternity, and in 1842 Wallace took his mother's maiden name.

In 1870 he inherited his father's collection, the château of Bagatelle, the apartment in the rue Laffitte, and the estates in Ireland. He also bought the lease of Hertford House from the 5th Marquess of Hertford. While Paris was besieged by the Prussians and then devastated by the uprising of the Commune, Wallace won a considerable reputation through charitable works and gifts to humanitarian causes. Among his donations were fifty drinking fountains to the city of Paris; a later example of the model is now in the drive of Hertford House. In recognition of his philanthropy he was made a baronet in 1871, just after he had married his mistress, Julie Castelnau, the mother of his thirty-year-old son, Edmond Richard.

In 1872 he took up residence in London, bringing with him from Paris many of his finest works of art, probably in the belief that they would there have a safer home. While Hertford House was being converted to accomm date them (1872-5), much of the collection was exhibited at the Bethnal Green Museum where it was a popular sensation, visited by five million people.

Unlike his father, Wallace took an interest in the responsibilities that his wealth brought him, particularly in Ireland. But the circumstances of his birth and the refusal of his wife and son to become anglicized meant that he was never fully accepted by English society. After the death of his son in 1887 he returned alone to Bagatelle where he died three years later in the same room as his father.

Wallace had been secretary to the 4th Marquess and, through acting as his agent, became a knowledgeable connoisseur. He bought many superb miniatures and gold boxes, but his taste in paintings, furniture and porcelain was similar to that of his father. He showed more independence in his taste for medieval and Renaissance works of art. In 1871 he purchased the collections of European arms and armour and medieval and Renaissance decorative arts formed by the comte de Nieuwerkerke, Napoleon III's Director of Fine Arts. In the same year he bought a selection of the arms and armour collected by Sir Samuel Meyrick and in 1872 he acquired the vicomte de Tauzia's early Italian paintings and illuminated manuscript cuttings. He bought very few works of art in the last fifteen years of his life.

Lady Wallace

Amélie Julie Charlotte Castelnau (1819-97) married Richard Wallace in 1871, having been his mistress for many years. She is said to have been an assistant in a perfumer's shop in Paris when they met.

In 1890 Sir Richard Wallace bequeathed to her all his property. There is no evidence that she had any enthusiasm for the great collection for which she then became responsible and, after Wallace's death, she led a secluded life at Hertford House. It was almost certainly the loyal desire to fulfil her husband's wishes that led her to leave the collection at Hertford House to the nation on her death. Wallace himself had discussed the idea with friends in the 1880s.

Lady Wallace, *c.* 1890

Sir John Murray Scott

There were still many superb pieces of eighteenth-century French furniture, sculpture and tapestry at the apartment in the rue Laffitte and at Bagatelle. These, together with the Lisburn estate in Ireland and the lease of Hertford House, Lady Wallace bequeathed to her secretary, John Murray Scott (1847-1912), who had been her principal adviser since Wallace's death. He was made a baronet in 1899.

Murray Scott sold the lease of Hertford House to the Government and became a Trustee of the Collection when it opened as a museum in 1900. He sold Bagatelle and many of the works of art that he had received in

Lady Wallace's will. On his death he left the considerable collection still remaining at the rue Laffitte apartment to his friend Lady Sackville of Knole. She sold this *en bloc* to a Parisian dealer and works of art from this part of the great collection formed by the Marquesses of Hertford and Sir Richard Wallace can now be found in museums and private collections throughout the world.

Hertford House

Hertford House was built as Manchester House in 1776-88 for the 4th Duke of Manchester. It was designed by Joshua Brown and was then much smaller than it is today, comprising only five bays, and with a Venetian window rather than the present conservatory on the first floor.

After a brief spell as the Spanish Embassy, it was leased in 1797 by the 2nd Marquess of Hertford who was apparently attracted by the good duckshooting available in the area. It was the 2nd Marquess who added the conservatory as well as two first-floor rooms on each wing. The Prince Regent, drawn by his infatuation for the 2nd Marchioness and his friendship with the 3rd Marquess,

Manchester House, later Hertford House, 1813

The Long Picture Gallery (now Gallery 22), *c*.1890

was a frequent visitor in the decade before his accession to the throne in 1820.

The house was leased as the French Embassy in 1836-50. But after 1850, under the 4th Marquess, it became little more than a store for his ever growing collection. In 1872 Sir Richard Wallace commissioned Thomas Ambler to undertake a major programme of alterations: an inner quadrangle was created with stabling, coach-houses and a Minton-tiled smoking room on the ground floor and top-lit galleries on the first floor; the wings of the house were raised to the full height of the central block and red brick replaced the stucco formerly on the facade.

In 1897-1900 the house was converted into a public museum. Exhibition galleries replaced the stabling, coach-houses and smoking room as well as some private rooms on the first floor. Many less radical changes have been made since then.

With the exception of the two great Caffiéri chandeliers in Galleries 4 and 5, all the chandeliers date from the nineteenth and twentieth centuries, although a few contain some eighteenth-century glass.

A Brief Visit to the Collection

Those visitors only able to make a brief visit might like to know that the medieval and Renaissance works of art and the armouries are on the ground floor and most of the old master paintings are on the first floor. Most of the finest French eighteenth-century paintings, furniture and porcelain can be found in Galleries 4, 16, 24 and 25. Gallery 22 contains many of the principal masterpieces (including Hals's *The Laughing Cavalier*).

Explanation

The following dates of French rulers may be useful:

Louis XIII	1610-43
Louis XIV	1643-1715
Régence	1715-23
Louis XV	1723-74
Louis XVI	1774-92
Napoleon I	1804-15
Louis XVIII	1815-24
Charles X	1824-30
Louis-Philippe	1830-48
Napoleon III	1852-70

In a guide of this kind it is only possible to include a selection of the finest works of art in each gallery. Detailed discussions of almost all the works of art in the Collection may be found in the relevant catalogues.

All references to individual items are accompanied by their inventory numbers to facilitate their identification and to accord with the catalogues. Those catalogues currently available are listed on p.94.

The function of each gallery in the time of Sir Richard Wallace and other relevant information about the fittings in his time have been indicated in italics after the gallery headings.

French School *c.*1715–20 *Madame de Ventadour with portraits of Louis XIV and his Heirs* (P122) detail

Entrance Hall

(The present staircase was installed in 1874; for the balustrade, see p.50. This area was returned to its appearance of c.1890 during the refurbishment of 1994/5.)

Nineteenth-century English paintings

LANDSEER: *The Arab Tent* (P376)

Landseer and his animal paintings were particularly admired by Queen Victoria. This picture, painted in 1866, was bought directly from the artist by her son, the Prince of Wales (later Edward VII), and then from him by Sir Richard Wallace. At over £7,800, it was the most expensive work of art ever bought for the Collection.

Gallery 1
Shop & Information

(Formerly the Breakfast Room)

Gallery 2

(Formerly the Billiard Room)

Furniture, paintings and sculpture from the Louis XIV and Régence periods

FRENCH SCHOOL *c.*1715-20: *Madame de Ventadour with portraits of Louis XIV and his Heirs* (P122)

P122 portrays the whole Bourbon dynasty: the bust on the left, Henri IV (1553-1610); the bust on the right, his son, Louis XIII (1601-43); seated, Louis XIII's eldest son, Louis XIV (1638-1715); standing left, Louis XIV's eldest son, Louis, the Grand Dauphin (1661-1711); standing right, his eldest son, Louis, duc de Bourgogne (1682-1712); and the latter's only surviving son, the infant duc d'Anjou, later Louis XV (1710-74). The other figure is Madame de Ventadour, the duc d'Anjou's governess, who saved his life during an epidemic of smallpox in 1712. The picture was probably painted for her.

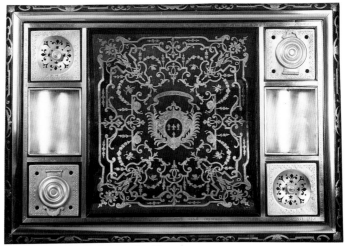

Attributed to Boulle Inkstand (F49)

BOULLE furniture

André-Charles Boulle was the most celebrated *ébéniste* (cabinet-maker) working under Louis XIV, perfecting (though not inventing) the technique of brass and tortoise-shell marquetry associated with his name. The impressive **wardrobe** (F429), with its fine *contre-partie* marquetry (where the design is of shell inlaid in brass), can be firmly attributed to Boulle since it corresponds with an armoire listed in his inventory of 1715. The superb **inkstand** (F49) was made in 1710 for the Paris Guild of Barber-Surgeons, whose motto and arms are incorporated within the elaborate marquetry design. Around the top edge are the names of some of the senior surgeons, including that of Georges Mareschal, who was first surgeon to Louis XIV. Phrases and symbols relating to medicine appear on the outer edges.

COYSEVOX: *Charles Le Brun* (S60)

Coysevox *Le Brun* (S60)

Le Brun (1619-90) was for many years a commanding figure in the French Academy. He was president in 1679 when Coysevox was admitted, the latter having offered as his reception piece a marble bust for which this terracotta (itself exhibited before the Academy in 1676) was the model. Coysevox had been *sculpteur du Roi* since 1666, and was extensively employed at the various royal châteaux. His fine bronze **bust** of Louis XIV (S165), also in this room, dates from *c*.1699.

Gallery 3
(Formerly the Dining Room)

Furniture and paintings from the Louis XV and Louis XVI periods

OUDRY: *The Dead Wolf* (P626) and *The Dead Roe* (P630)

Oudry, who specialized in animal and game pieces in the Dutch and Flemish tradition, received many commissions from European courts. He also made numerous tapestry designs, becoming director of the manufactories of Beauvais (1734) and the Gobelins (1748). P626 and P630, both of 1721, were painted as a pair and are among his finest works. (For Oudry see also Gallery 4.)

CARLIN: *Table à pupitre* (F327)

As ingenious as it is beautiful, F327 combines a work, writing and reading-table, and is veneered with tulipwood and mounted with five fine Sèvres porcelain **plaques** (C506) painted by BOUILLIAT in 1783. Concealed within are two drawers, a candle-stand at each side and a mechanism allowing the entire top to be raised and tilted to form a book-rest. As Carlin (master 1766) died in 1785, this must have been one of his last pieces. He also made the Sèvres-mounted **secretaire** (F304), veneered with tulip- and purplewoods, the central **plaque** (C502) again painted by BOUILLIAT and dated 1776.

Sèvres porcelain Plaque (C506a) from Carlin *Table à pupitre* (F327)

NATTIER: *Mademoiselle de Clermont en sultane* (P456)

This painting, dated 1733, fancifully depicts Mademoiselle de Clermont (1697-1741) at her bath amid attendants and accessories in the Turkish style. It typifies the fashion for *turqueries* popular at that time in France (see also C. VAN LOO: *The Grand Turk giving a Concert to his Mistress* (P451) in this room). Her husband, the duc de Joyeuse, was killed in a hunting accident within a few days of their marriage in 1724, and their tragic romance became the basis for a once popular novel, *Mlle de Clermont* by Madame de Genlis.

Gallery 4

(Formerly the Back State Room; refurbished in 1995/6)

Furniture, Sèvres porcelain and paintings from the Louis XV period

In this room have been gathered many of the most extra-ordinary pieces of Sèvres porcelain and furniture in the Collection from the Louis XV period, representing the rococo style at its most opulent and spectacular.

Sèvres porcelain

Under the influence of Madame de Pompadour, the French royal porcelain factory moved from Vincennes to Sèvres in 1756, and was bought by Louis XV in 1759. Until the secret ingredient (kaolin) of Chinese and Meissen hard-paste porcelain was discovered in the 1760s, Sèvres could only make the more vulnerable and costly soft-paste variety. Each piece had to be moulded or thrown, fired, and then fired again after separate applications of glaze, colour and gilding. All the Sèvres porcelain in this unrivalled museum collection of over 300 pieces was made between 1752 and 1794, representing the vast range of models and decorations of the eighteenth century.

The pair of **vases with candleholders** '*à tête d'éléphant*' (C246-7), made in 1756, typifies the extraordinary imagi-nation of the designers at the Sèvres factory, led by the chief designer, JEAN-CLAUDE DUPLESSIS *père* (*c*.1695-1774). The delicate painting is by DODIN, perhaps the finest of the painters at Sèvres. Later models, such as C249-50, required the addition of supporting handles under the vulnerable trunks; these **vases** formed a garniture with a **pot-pourri vase** (C248), and were possibly bought by

Sèvres porcelain Vase '*à tête d'élephant*' (D246) detail

Madame de Pompadour in 1759. In the same year, Louis XV himself probably acquired the splendid blue and green ground **garniture of three vases** (C251-3). The fine painted reserves, depicting military encampments, are attributed to MORIN (see detail of C251 on back cover).

Régulateur (Astronomical) Clock (F98)

The monumental scale, elaborate decoration and complex movement of F98 make it one of the most remarkable clocks produced in eighteenth-century France. It was made *c.*1750 for the financier Jean Paris de Monmartel (godfather to Madame de Pompadour), who was portrayed with it in an engraving of 1772. The movement was designed by FORTIER and made by STOLLEWERCK; the patinated-bronze figures are possibly by J. CAFFIÉRI (who signed the fine **chandelier** (F84) in this room; see also Gallery 5). The principal clock-face now shows Greenwich mean time (blued-steel hand) and apparent solar time (gilt hand); from the central dial can be read the passage of the sun across the Zodiac, the age, longitude and phases of the moon, and the time anywhere in the northern hemisphere (a map of which is engraved on the revolving circular plate); the two lowest dials show the rising and setting of the sun (left) and moon (right).

Régulateur (Astronomical) Clock (F98) detail

Gaudreaus Chest of Drawers (F86)

GAUDREAUS: Chest of Drawers (F86)

This piece of furniture is of the highest importance. It was made in 1739 for the bedchamber of Louis XV at Versailles and originally stood under a mirror which still survives in the panelling of the walls of the room. Based on a drawing by one of the SLODTZ BROTHERS, it was made by Gaudreaus with mounts by J. CAFFIÉRI (for whom, see below). With its double-bowed front and lavish mounts, the chest of drawers demonstrates the transition which took place in French furniture in the 1720s and 1730s away from the monumental style associated with A.-C. Boulle (see Gallery 2) towards more graceful and flowing forms. The marquetry is in kingwood and *satiné*.

Copy of the Roll-Top Desk '*Le Bureau du Roi Louis XV*' (F460)

The magnificent original desk (now at Versailles) was begun by OEBEN (*ébéniste du Roi* 1754) and completed in 1769 by his pupil RIESENER (*ébéniste du Roi* 1774) for Louis XV. It was one of the earliest roll-top desks ever made and the most expensive piece of furniture produced in eighteenth-century France. It also established Riesener's reputation, even though Oeben was responsible for much of the design and details. F460 was commissioned by the 4th Marquess and copies the mid-nineteenth-century appearance of the original: during the Revolution its royal emblems had been replaced by attributes of the Arts (in marquetry on the roll-top) and its royal ciphers by Wedgwood-style Sèvres plaques (at the sides).

JACOB: Set of six arm-chairs, with two sofas (F185-92)

These fine chairs are stamped with the mark of Georges Jacob, the most eminent chair-maker of the Louis XVI period. They are covered with Louis XV Beauvais tapestry, probably applied in the nineteenth century when the two sofas were made to match them. The various scenes of animals are taken from designs by OUDRY, who in 1748 painted as overdoors the set of four animal subjects in this room (P625, P627, P629 and P631).

Gallery 5

(Formerly the Front State Room, and refurbished as such in 1994/5)

Eighteenth & nineteenth-century English portraits, furniture and Sèvres porcelain of the Louis XV and Louis XVI periods

Gallery 5

24

HOPPNER: *George IV as Prince of Wales* (P563)

This portrait was painted in about 1792 when the Prince was thirty years old (a portrait of him by Lawrence in Gallery 22 shows him thirty years later as King). In 1810 it was given by the Prince (who specially commissioned the frame) to the Earl of Yarmouth, later 3rd Marquess of Hertford, his Vice-Chamberlain and sale-room adviser. The Prince at that time was also enjoying a liaison with the 2nd Marchioness of Hertford.

LAWRENCE: *Margaret, Countess of Blessington* (P558)

Painted in 1822, this portrait of a fashionable literary hostess is one of the artist's most compelling characterisations. Byron, whom the Countess later met in Italy, wrote that it had 'set all London raving' when first exhibited. The Countess (who had lived briefly in Manchester Square) was obliged to sell all her possessions in 1849, and died shortly afterwards in Paris.

CAFFIÉRI: *Chandelier* (F84)

Jacques Caffiéri, one of a long dynasty of prominent sculptors and *fondeurs* (bronze founders), was much employed in the latter capacity by the French Crown. This chandelier, and the even more elaborate example (F83) in Gallery 4, were probably presented by Louis XV to his eldest daughter, Madame Louise-Elisabeth, in 1752 or 1753. They are exceptional examples of the rococo style, of which Caffiéri was a leading exponent.

Musical Clock (F96)

Like the similar musical clock (F97) in Gallery 4, the gilt-bronze case of F96 was perhaps designed by Duplessis *père*, and has a carillon of fourteen bells. The movement of F96 was made by DAILLÉ, and the carillon, which can play fourteen different tunes, by STOLLEWERCK.

Hoppner *George IV as Prince of Wales* (P503)

Sèvres porcelain Ice-cream Cooler (C478)

Sèvres Porcelain

The magnificent **wine** and **ice-cream coolers** (C474, C476-7) were part of an 800-piece dinner service in the neo-classical style made at vast expense for Empress Catherine II of Russia in 1778-9; over 2,200 pieces had to be rejected after firing damage. In 1837, over 100 pieces from the service were looted after a fire at the Hermitage. The 4th Marquess later acquired many of them; he kept the six most elaborate for himself (the three other pieces are in Gallery 16), providing them with lavish gilt-bronze mounts, and then sold the remainder back to the Tsar.

Pilon *Charles IX of France* (S154)

Gallery 6
(Formerly two rooms: the Canaletto Room and the Sixteenth Century Room)

Medieval, Renaissance and Baroque works of art

Almost all the objects shown in Galleries 6 and 7 were collected by Sir Richard Wallace. His taste reflects the later nineteenth-century revival of the princely Renaissance enthusiasm for displaying together curiosities and works of art of a widely disparate nature.

PILON: *Charles IX of France* (S154)

Pilon, whose style reflects Italianate influences, was perhaps the most important sculptor of late sixteenth-century France; as *sculpteur du Roi*, he worked on many royal commissions. In this superb bronze bust Charles IX (1550-74) is lent dignity and status by the classical laurel-wreath and *armour à l'antique* - in reality he was feeble and undistinguished.

Wax Miniatures (case 2)

Wax portraits and statuettes as works of art in their own right (rather than models for cast bronzes) became popular in the courtly circles of France and Italy in the early sixteenth-century. The diptych of the *Duc de Guise and his wife* (S417) which dates from that time is one of the earliest of its kind to survive. Later waxes include *Archduke Ernst of Austria* (S434) by ANTONIO ABONDIO, a late sixteenth-century Milanese medallist; *Ulrich, Grundherr von Altenthann and Weiherhauss* (S449) of 1627 by GEORG HOLD-ERMANN of Nuremburg; and *Susannah and the Elders* (S460) by DANIEL NEUBERGER of Augsburg (1621-80).

Illuminated manuscript cuttings (case 3)

These were cut from medieval and Renaissance manuscripts and framed in the nineteenth century. They range in date from the Pisan **initials** (M344), of the 1330s, to the French mid sixteenth-century Garden of Love scene (M323). Of particular quality are *Galeazzo Sforza in prayer* (M342), by CRISTOFORO DA PREDA (Milan, 1477), and the two scenes from *Boëthius* (M320-1), attributed to the MAÎTRE DE COËTIVY (French, 1460s).

Limoges enamel
Parnassus Dish
(III F 268)

Limoges painted enamels (case B)

The process of painted enamelling was developed at Limoges in the late-fifteenth century. The copper object was covered with a ground of enamel (a type of leaded glass), fired once, and then the different colours were each painted on and fired separately. The brilliance of the colours was often enhanced by the use of metal foil beneath the translucent enamel. Leading painters of the sixteenth century included the PÉNICAUD family, LÉONARD LIMOUSIN, PIERRE REYMOND and JEAN DE COURT - all represented here. Their designs were generally closely copied from contemporary engravings and woodcuts (see, for example, the series of 24 **plaques** (III F 250) after Dürer's *Small Passion* woodcuts). Especially attractive are the impressive *Parnassus* **dish** (III F 268) by MARTIAL COURTOIS, and the charming **tazza** (III F 267) depicting *Noah's Ark* by JEAN DE COURT.

TORRIGIANO: *Head of Christ* (S7)

Pietro Torrigiano, who had been a student with Michelangelo in the Florentine Academy, produced effigies of Henry VII and his Queen for Westminster Abbey

29

in 1511-18. This bust was also sculpted for the Abbey, and was originally mounted on a wall between the Islip and Esteney Chapels in the north transept. It was probably removed from this location in the eighteenth century.

FOPPA: *The Young Cicero Reading* (P538)

Painted *c*.1464 by the principal Lombard artist of the time, this is the only surviving fresco from the Palazzo Mediceo, Milan (aquired by Cosimo de' Medici in 1455). It was set in an open courtyard for four hundred years before being cut down and framed, hence its poor condition. Cicero, the great Roman orator, had excelled at school, and this choice of subject reflects the Renaissance interest in classical learning.

Glass (case C)

Glass Chalice (XXV B 96)

Most pieces in the collection were made in Venice, or in the Venetian manner, in the sixteenth and seventeenth centuries. The principal techniques using colourless glass (*cristallo*), opaque white canes (*vetro a filigrana*), mould-blowing and ice-glass are represented, and there is a good range of decorative methods, including enamelling, gilding, engraving and applied reliefs. Three particularly fine sixteenth-century pieces are the 'chalcedony' **goblet** (XXV B 92), a trick **glass** (XXV B 72) with a mould-blown lion (both Venetian), and the French **chalice** (XXV B 96). The earliest object is the Syrian **mosque lamp** (XXV B 94), probably dating from the 1350s.

Gallery 7

(Formerly the Smoking Room; until 1937, Minton-tiled throughout)

Medieval, Renaissance and Baroque works of art

Coins and medals (case 1)

PISANELLO, who designed the medal of *Gianfrancesco Gonzaga* (S328), *c*.1444, was the first medallist since the classical period, and one of the greatest. Other important portrait medals include: *Sigismondo Malatesta* (S329) by MATTEO DEI PASTI (Verona, 1446); *Desiderius Erasmus* (S401) by MASSYS (Antwerp, 1519); and *The Emperor Charles V* (S400) by DÜRER (Nuremberg, 1521).

Gallery 8
Renaissance arms and armour, firearms and edged weapons sixteenth to nineteenth century

Edged weapons

In addition to the fine displays of sixteenth and seventeenth-century swept-hilt **rapiers**, there are some very fine eighteenth-century **'dress' swords** and **smallswords** (mainly in case 5); these include one (A672) with an exceptional chiselled and gilt hilt by CASPAR SPÄT, who worked for the Bavarian court. Case H contains several later seventeenth-century civilian swords, the style of which marks the transition between the rapier and smallsword. A particularly interesting military weapon is the Spanish **fighting sword** (A695), in case F. This is inscribed on the hilt 'San Josef Feby.14 1797', indicating that it was probably surrendered from the warship of that name when the latter was captured by Horatio Nelson at the Battle of Cape St Vincent. Among the fine range of **daggers** are some exotic specialized examples such as spring-loaded triple-bladed **left-hand daggers**, and saw-toothed **'sword-breakers'** (case A, right). There are also a number of sixteenth-century **'Landsknecht' daggers**, named after a ferocious and flamboyant class of German mercenaries; one of their fearsome **two-handed swords** (A470) is in case B. The nearby *'Sword of Justice'* (A721) is of the type used as a **headsman's sword**, and in a ceremonial role would have symbolized the authority of judges over life and death. Some of the decorated weapons (especially the **hunting swords and knives** in case 6) were intended less for use than as works of art; particularly splendid is that given by Napoleon III to the 4th Marquess of Hertford (A707), in case 4. It is of solid silver, cast and chased, depicting an American Indian fighting two mountain lions.

Projectile weapons

Many of the predominantly sixteenth-century **wheellock firearms** were obtained by Sir Richard Wallace from the enterprising Parisian dealer Frédéric Spitzer who specialized in assembling or redecorating such weapons to suit the taste of his wealthy clientele (see case 1).

Outstanding among the unaltered wheel-lock guns is the magnificent **sporting gun** (A1090) in case 2 by DANIEL SADELER of Munich, with a stock by HIERONYMOUS BORSTORFFER. This was probably made for the Bavarian Electoral court in c.1620. The **pistol** by JEAN LE BOUR-GEOIS (A1176) in case 2, and the **wheel-lock guns** in case 2 (A1110) and in case A (A1111), all came from the Armoury of Louis XIII, a noted sportsman and gun-collector. Many of the important group of fine quality eighteenth-century guns in case 4 also have an impressive provenance: the silver-mounted **flint-lock blunder-buss** (A1124), made by J. A. GRECKE of St Petersburg in 1780, bears the monogram of Catherine the Great; and the magnificent **French sporting guns** by NICOLAS-NOËL BOUTET (A1128-9) were once owned by Charles IV of Spain, but were seized by his usurper Joseph Bonaparte, who applied his coat of arms to one of them. In case A there is a particularly fine **double-barrelled flint-lock** rifle, cased with all its accessories, made by BOUTET; it bears the monogram of Tsar Nicholas I of Russia (A1126). Some of the many pistols in case 5 are similarly important; one pair of especially ornate **flint-lock pistols** (A1209-10) was made for Louis XIV as a gift from the City of Lille, to mark its own annexation and other French military successes in the Spanish Netherlands during the campaign of 1667-8.

Armour

In the centre of the gallery is the impressive blacked, etched and gilt **equestrian harness** (A29) made by HANS RINGLER of Nuremberg for Otto Heinrich, Count Palatine of the Rhine (1502-59); it is in fact composed of pieces from more than one 'garniture' (see Gallery 9).

Most of the other armours in the wall cases date from the sixteenth and early seventeenth centuries. The late sixteenth-century Nuremberg black and white **munition armours** (A40-2) were worn by ordinary infantry soldiers, and the series of **'morion' helmets** of similar date (A114-8), in case G, were made for the Saxon Electoral Guard. The increasing effectiveness of firearms in battle led to the gradual abandonment of full plate armour; the **'cuirassier' armour** (A65) in case H, South German, c.1620, marks its final form. The small dent in the $11\frac{1}{4}$lbs (5kg) breastplate is a mark of the proof of that piece against shot. The richly etched and gilt Italian **armour** (A63) of c.1600-10, in case E, although of similar form was made as a parade armour for a prince of the House of Savoy; its breastplate, weighing only $7\frac{3}{4}$ lbs (3.5kg), would probably not have been shot-proof.

Works of art

The very fine walnut **coffer** in case A, inlaid with stag's horn, mother-of-pearl and brass (A1345), is signed by the Alsatian gunstock-maker J.-C. TORNIER, and dated 1630. He probably made and decorated the stock of the **wheel-lock rifle** (A1099) in case 2, dated 1645.

Gallery 9
Renaissance arms and armour

Edged weapons

In case 1 is a very fine combined **wheel-lock pistol** and **swept-hilt rapier** (A1241) made in Augsburg c.1580-90. Most of the swords in the Collection are German or Italian, but the hilt of the silver-encrusted **cross-hilted sword** (A511) in case 4 is English, probably by ROBERT SOUTH of London. Its blade is by the German CLEMENS HORN. This rare dress sword was made for Henry, Prince of Wales (d.1612), who predeceased both his father, James I, and his younger brother, Charles I.

During the seventeenth century in Spain, and to a certain extent in Spanish-dominated Italy also, the **'cup-hilted' rapier** became fashionable in place of the earlier 'swept' form; a superb example (A655) in case 2, dated 1701, has a fine chiselled hilt signed by ESTRADA of Madrid, and a blade by FRANCISCO GOMEZ of Toledo. In case H are

South and Horn Sword of Henry, Prince of Wales (A511) detail

several ornately pierced and chiselled Spanish or Italian **left-hand daggers** (swords were usually held in the right hand, daggers in the left). More common in Northern Europe were **'quillon' daggers**; a particularly notable one in case 3 (A790) was given to Henri IV of France by the City of Paris upon the occasion of his marriage to Marie de Médicis in 1600; its companion rapier (now in the Musée de l'Armée, Paris) was carried by Napoleon on his campaigns throughout Europe as a symbol of good luck.

Projectile weapons

Especially fine is the cast and chased bronze **cannon barrel** (A1245), signed and dated 1688 by F. MAZZAROLI of Venice. Its impressive carriage was made in 1853-4 for Anatole Demidoff, Prince of San Donato, at whose sale in 1870 it was bought by the 4th Marquess of Hertford.

Armour

The Gothic **war harnesss** for man and horse (A21) dominates this room; although restored in the nineteenth century and partly composite, its elegant form and shell-like fluting are characteristic of German fifteenth-century armour at its best. It was probably made for a member of the Bavarian von Freyberg family c.1470-90. The sixteenth-century armour ranges in date from the German 'Maximilian' style (A24) in case B to the richly ornamented Italian parade armour (A51) in case F. The three Augsburg **tilt armours** (A47-9) in case G, made in the late 1580s, are probably all from the workshop of ANTON PEFFENHAUSER.

Gothic Harness for man and horse (A21)

Garnitures

In the sixteenth century it became fashionable to build one armour to which 'exchange' pieces could be added, substituted or removed, either to alter its function (between war, parade, and various forms of the tournament) or as reinforcement. Over the centuries many such garnitures have been dispersed, and several fine pieces are now in this Collection. In case 4 there is an etched and gilt **helmet** for tournament on foot (A188) from the 'Golden Garniture' made for the Emperor Ferdinand I in 1555. Adjacent are the **helmet, pauldron** (shoulder armour) and **vamplate** (for the lance) from an Augsburg garniture made *c.*1575 for the Emperor Maximilian II's two sons (AA187, A242, A343). A **gauntlet** (A270) is part of another Augsburg garniture, made for Maximilian in 1550 by MATTHÄUS FRAUENPREIS and etched by JÖRG SORG. A further garniture made for Maximilian, in 1571, is represented by a **shaffron** (headpiece for a horse) (A359) and **vamplate** (A342). The **embossed shield** (A320), from a garniture made *c.*1556-9 for Henri II, is French, with decoration after designs by ETIENNE DELAUNE; while a right-hand **gauntlet** (A276) was made *c.*1608 at Greenwich (probably by JACOB HALDER) for Henry, Prince of Wales. The suit to which it belongs is in the Royal Collection at Windsor Castle. The only complete harness of English plate armour here is in case C (A62), the superb Greenwich **field garniture** made *c.*1587 probably for Thomas Sackville, Lord Buckhurst, later 1st Earl of Dorset.

Gallery 10
Medieval and Renaissance arms and armour

Edged weapons

The display case C illustrates, from right to left, the development of the **sword** from the simple cross-hilt as in the tenth-century North European example (A456), to the sixteenth-century 'developed' hilt, such as A480 with its more complex guard. Especially fine are the Renaissance swords and daggers in case 2 in the centre of the gallery: the **hunting sword** (*falchion*) A710 came from the Armoury of the Medici. The **dagger** A743 is one of a number of rare fifteenth-century Italian *cinquedea* (having blades of 'five fingers' breadth'); it retains its original sheath of *cuir bouilli* (tooled hardened leather).

Many of the arms have a noble provenance. In case 1, for example, there is the fifteenth-century **serving-knife** (A881) of Philip the Good, Duke of Burgundy, richly enamelled with his coat of arms. There is also an impressive range of staff weapons, of which the finest is probably the **pollaxe** (A926) in case C, made c.1450-70. The motto 'de bon' in a heart (i.e. 'of good heart') is incised into the decorative brass inlay of the head. Pollaxes such as this were commonly used in tournaments when fighting on foot, but were doubtless also used in battle.

Projectile weapons

In case 1 is a magnificent late fifteenth-century **crossbow** (A1032) which once belonged to the Völs Colonna family in the Tyrol. The tiller is overlaid with plaques of carved staghorn to resemble ivory, while the bow is in steel (an early example of its use) covered with painted and gilded parchment. A weapon as fine as this would have been used for ostentatious display in the hunt, rather than for war. Later crossbows are in Gallery 8 (case A), together with a selection of bolts or quarrels, as their arrows were called.

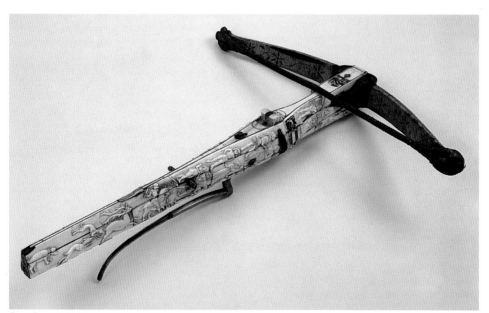

Crossbow (A1032)

41

Great Helm (A186)

Armour

Particularly fine and rare pieces of armour in this Gallery include the Milanese **basinet** (helmet) made *c*.1390-1410 (A69), case 4, and the pair of late fourteenth-century 'hour-glass' **gauntlets** (A251-2), case 3, with incised decoration incorporating the motto 'Amor' (Love). Of similar rarity, made from only two pieces of entirely hand-forged iron, is the early fifteenth-century frog-mouthed **great helm** (A186) in the same case. Nearby in case F is the heaviest **tilt armour** (A23) in the Collection, weighing 96lbs (43kg). It dates from the early sixteenth century, and was possibly made for the Nuremberg tournaments, its surface bearing ample evidence of its use. Armour like this was quite unsuited for war; a lighter **armour**, more appropriate for the battlefield but, with the addition of exchange pieces, also suitable for use in a tournament, stands next to it (A22) in case G. It was probably made for Wladislas, King of Poland and Hungary, *c*.1510. Later Renaissance armour fashioned in a more ornate style is also to be found here (and in Gallery 9). The **visor** (A204) in case B, embossed into the form of a grotesque Turk's face, is from a helmet made by Hans Seusenhofer for the future Emperor Ferdinand I in 1529. The Italian **parade helmets** in case 2 are of a similar date and are attributed to famous craftsmen such as the NEGROLI BROTHERS of Milan and CAREMOLO MODRONE of Mantua.

The stairs lead to Gallery 23.

Mughal Indian Dagger (OA1409)

Gallery 11
Oriental arms, armour and works of art. Also French Orientalist paintings

Nearly all the Oriental arms, armour and works of art were acquired by the 4th Marquess of Hertford in 1860-70, a period when objects of this kind were highly fashionable in Parisian society. They were regarded as suitable for wall displays and as works of art.

Edged weapons

Most of the edged weapons are Indian and Persian, with some Turkish and Far Eastern examples in cases C and G. Of special interest are the daggers in case 6, particularly the jewelled and gold-hilted Mughal Indian **dagger** (OA1409) dating from the early seventeenth century, and

Indian Tulwar of Tipu Sultan (OA1402)

the Persian example (OA1414) with its gold encrusted blade dated 1496-7. The fine collection of swords includes an Indian **tulwar** once owned by Tipu Sultan of Mysore (OA1402) in case B; its jade hilt is inlaid with gold, diamonds, rubies and emeralds, and its fine seventeenth-century Persian blade bears the badge of Tipu (a tiger) damascened in gold. The **sword** of Ranjit Singh, founder of the Sikh dynasty in the Punjab (OA1404), may be seen in case 5. Also worth noting is the superb fifteenth-century Japanese **sword blade** (OA1694) in case F.

Armour

The armour is predominantly eighteenth and nineteenth-century Indian and Persian, of steel decorated with gold in a technique known as *cuftgari*, in which the gold is applied and burnished on to a finely cross-hatched ground. In Europe this work was known as 'counterfeit damascening' because the gold was not laid into a groove cut to receive it, as in 'true' damascening. Especially impressive is the nineteenth-century Imperial **court dress** of a Chinese Mandarin (OA1701) in case A, and between the doors into Gallery 10, the standing figures in case H, illustrating the **war panoply** of an Indian Rajput warrior (OA1790-4). The latter incorporates a rare late eighteenth-century 'Coat of Ten Thousand Nails', so-called because of its many gilt studs. Few similar pieces have survived because of the fragility of the textile elements.

Projectile weapons

Displayed in cases D and E, the richly decorated matchlock and flintlock firearms were designed not only for conspicuous display and as prestigious gifts for Eastern potentates but often also for use. The multi-shot revolving **matchlock carbine** (OA2202), case E, with a hand-turned cylinder capable of holding six charges, was made in India in the late seventeenth century. The unusual eighteenth-century **matchlock gun** (OA2003) from Bhutan is a purpose-designed hunting weapon, fitted with a hinged bi-pod support for steady, accurate shooting. In contrast, the **flintlock blunderbuss** (OA2086), case D, can only have been used for show; its touch-hole has never been drilled, and it therefore cannot be fired.

Works of art

Of special note in case 6 is the rare Indian or Persian **dish and cover** (OA1662) of richly enamelled gold, signed in Persian by the maker and dated 1811. The West African Asante **gold treasure** (OA1673-83), in the centre of the gallery, case 4, was bought by Sir Richard Wallace following a charitable auction for the widows and orphans of soldiers who fought in the 1874 Asante campaign.

VERNET: *The Arab Tale-teller* (P280)

French nineteenth-century interest in the lands and culture of the Arabs was greatly stimulated by the conquest of Algeria in 1830. Vernet paid four visits to Algeria, where he understood the Arab way of life to be a survival from Biblical times (see *Judah and Tamar* (P326) and *Joseph's Coat* (P349) in Gallery 23). He also produced many

Vernet *The Arab Tale-teller* (P280)

Orientalist pictures without Biblical reference, of which the *Arab Tale-teller*, painted in 1833, was the first to be exhibited at the Salon. The 4th Marquess knew Vernet well and admired his works; there are twenty-nine of his oils and watercolours in the Collection.

DECAMPS: *The Turkish Patrol* (P307)

Turkish themes had been common in eighteenth-century French art (see Nattier's *Mademoiselle de Clermont* in Gallery 15) and they became part of a more general Oriental taste in the nineteenth century. Decamps visited the Middle East and North Africa in 1828 and thereafter painted numerous Oriental scenes, usually in a heavily impasted technique that has not lasted well. *The Turkish Patrol*, showing nine men of a foot-patrol accompanying the chief of police on his round in Smyrna, was Decamps's first major Oriental subject. With Horace Vernet, he was one of the 4th Marquess of Hertford's favourite artists and there are twenty-eight of his paintings and watercolours in the Collection.

Boucher *The Rising of the Sun* (P485)

BOUCHER: *An Autumn Pastoral* (P482) and *A Summer Pastoral* (P489)

Boucher painted these pendant scenes in 1749 for the financier Trudaine's new château at Montigny-Lencoup. Their subjects derive from *pantomines* by his friend Favart (for whom he sometimes devised theatrical settings). They are his largest and arguably his finest theatrical pastorals. Two other paintings derived from Favart's plays are in Galleries 24 (P399) and 13 (P431). Three further pairs of paintings by Boucher hang on the Landing.

Gallery 13

(Formerly Lady Wallace's boudoir)

English and French paintings reflecting the eighteenth-century cult of sensibility. Also Louis XV and Louis XVI furniture

Together with the writings of Rousseau and the novelist Samuel Richardson, the most influential expressions of the eighteenth-century cult of sensibility were the paintings of Jean-Baptiste Greuze. His sentimental and moral scenes were intended to evoke tender feelings in the heart of the viewer and introduced a new sentimentality into French painting. Reynolds and Morland reflect the same attitude in English painting. Reynolds in particular admired Greuze's pictures and they may have influenced some of his compositions.

GREUZE: *The Inconsolable Widow* (P454) and
The Broken Mirror (P442)

These two pictures were both painted in 1762-3 and offer examples of virtue and vice. The young widow rereads old letters and vows fidelity to her husband while her grieving dog lies in dejection at her feet. In *The Broken Mirror* the disorder of the room suggests the intemperence of the girl, while the shattered mirror indicates her lost virginity.

GREUZE: *Innocence* (P384)

Greuze painted many heads of children (*têtes d'expression*). Perhaps no pictures illustrate better the differences in taste between our time and that of the eighteenth and nineteenth centuries when these works were hugely popular. Sexual allusions are undoubtedly contained within

Greuze *The Broken Mirror* (P442)

some of his pictures of young girls, but there is no reason to doubt that the title of this work was accepted as entirely genuine by most viewers in the nineteenth century when it became one of the most reproduced pictures in the world. *Innocence* was the most expensive of the 4th Marquess of Hertford's eighteenth-century French pictures. He had a great enthusiasm for Greuze's heads of children and there are thirteen still in the Collection today (also in Galleries 15 and 24).

REYNOLDS: *The Strawberry Girl* (P40)

This is a 'fancy picture' (i.e. a pleasing study of a figure, usually a child, in fancy dress) rather than a portrait, and as such is a characteristic work of the age of sensibility. The identity of the child is unknown. Exhibited at the Royal Academy in 1773, the picture was regarded by Reynolds as one of his best works and the many repititions produced in his studio testify to its popularity.

DUBOIS: Writing-table, inkstand and *cartonnier* (F330, F287 and F178)

All three pieces are lacquered with green *vernis Martin*, a substance made in imitation of Oriental lacquer using many coats of coloured varnish which (like Oriental lacquer itself) were rubbed down and polished after each application. The name derives from the brothers Martin who perfected but did not invent the process. These pieces were made in Paris *c.*1765, possibly for Catherine II of Russia.

WEISWEILER: Work-table (F325)

The early history of this work-table, for use by a lady engaged in sewing or some similar domestic occupation, is unknown. It was probably made in the 1780s, but it is first recorded in 1807 in the apartments of the Empress Josephine at the Tuileries in Paris. Its grace and delicacy reflect both its intended use and its date. Under Louis XVI lighter and smaller pieces of furniture for use by ladies became fashionable. The Wedgwood plaques were probably imported by the fashionable shopkeeper Daguerre, for whom Weisweiler frequently worked. Wedgwood's designs and products were popular and influential in France.

Weisweiler Work-table (F325)

Corridor

In the two cases in the corridor between Galleries 13 and 14 are displayed, among other items, gold boxes, a perpetual almanach and a silver-gilt service.

Gold boxes

In the eighteenth century the taking of snuff was a fashionable activity enjoyed by women as well as men. Most of the gold boxes in the Collection were intended for snuff but they were also extravagant toys for the very rich, as much designed for display as for use. Superb works of craftsmanship, they kept their contents fresh only by the precision of the fit of box and lid, and do not have catches. They can also be held perfectly balanced in the hand with the lid raised.

Most of the gold boxes in the Collection are French but there are also important examples from Germany, Austria, Switzerland and England. There are boxes decorated entirely in gold, either plain or four-colour (achieved by adding other metals like silver or iron to the gold), but most have painted decoration, either on enamel, gouache, gold foil or porcelain. Glass, Japanese lacquer, tortoiseshell and mother-of-pearl were also used. The 4th Marquess of Hertford bought some of the boxes, but most seem to have been acquired by Sir Richard Wallace.

Gold box (G80) with *Portrait of the Marquise du Châtelet*

One of the most interesting boxes, G80, made in gold and a hardstone called cornelian, has a secret panel, rediscovered only in 1976, showing on each side gouache portraits of Voltaire and his mistress, the marquise du Châtelet. It was made in Dresden in *c*.1770-5.

In the display case the visitor may also notice some beautifully made drizzling shuttles, used for winding gold thread removed from dresses so that the gold could be used again.

MARTINIÈRE: Perpetual Almanach (F64)

This almanach in four parts was made for Louis XV in 1741-2. It is made of enamel on copper, painted on a white ground and framed with gilt bronze. The slips of enamel indicate the days of the week and the phases of the moon as well as the date and the names of the various

Attributed to Boulle Wardrobe (F61)

feast days. The appropriate sign of the zodiac is also indicated. The back of each panel is removable to allow the slips to be adjusted annually.

Silver-gilt Service

This service was made (with its fitted leather case, not on display) by several craftsmen at Augsburg between 1757 and 1773. Comprising fifty-five pieces, the service can be divided into three parts: a toilet-service, a breakfast-service and a writing-set. It was probably made for a lady of high rank, but her identity is unknown.

Gallery 14
(Formerly Sir Richard Wallace's Study)
Fine Boulle Furniture; seventeenth-century Dutch and Spanish paintings

BOULLE furniture

The imposing **wardrobe** (F61) of *c*.1695, similar to F62 in Gallery 16, can be firmly attributed to the Boulle workshop. The central door-panels are veneered with *première-partie* marquetry (brass inlaid in tortoiseshell) and mounted with gilt-bronze groups of *Apollo and Daphne* (left) and *The Flaying of Marsyas* (right). The rigorous symmetry of the piece is emphasized by the repetition on the inner edges of the hinge-mounts, whose *fleurs de lis* suggest a royal provenance (the royal monogram is also cast behind the keyhole escutcheons). In the centre of the room stands a fine **writing-table** (F427), probably made in the Boulle workshop a little before the lovely **toilet mirror** (F50). This was made in 1713 as part of a service for the duchesse de Berry, and later passed to Charlotte, princesse de Chimay, whose arms it now bears. The marquetry on the back is after an engraving by Jean Berain, the King's designer, who popularised designs such as this of *singeries* (monkeys, often dressed in clothes and imitating human actions). The Boulle workshop also made the splendid **pedestal clock** (F42) mounted with figures representing the four continents of (from the left) Africa, Europe, Asia and America. The clock movement is by MYNUÈL; other examples of this clock have an oval dial with hands that expand and contract correspondingly.

Attributed to DROST: *The Unmerciful Servant* (P86)
Although accepted as a fine work by Rembrandt in the nineteenth century, this picture is now attributed to his pupil Willem Drost. It probably shows the moment in the Parable of the Unmerciful Servant when the king condemns one of his servants who had heartlessly extracted a debt from another, although a different Biblical subject, the Centurion Cornelius, has also been suggested. Drost's *Portrait of a young Woman* (P61) can be seen in Gallery 18.

VAN DER HELST: *A Family Group* (P110)
By the mid-1640s van der Helst had become the most fashionable portrait painter in Amsterdam, ousting Rembrandt from this position. His clear colour and smooth technique particularly appealed to prosperous sitters such as the unidentified couple shown here with their daughter. This hunting portrait was painted in 1654, soon after hunting had ceased to be the exclusive preserve of the nobility. Newly affluent sections of Dutch society were keen to display the privileges they had recently acquired.

Gallery 15
(Formerly the Oval Drawing Room; this is the only room to retain its original fireplace)
Late eighteenth-century French furniture, sculpture and paintings

GREUZE: *Votive offering to Cupid* (P441)
Despite his success with sentimental genre, Greuze had serious ambitions as a history painter, the noblest category of painting according to the eighteenth-century hierarchy of subject matter maintained by the French Academy. This is one of several classical subjects he painted in the late-1760s, and the details of architecture, altar and ewer, reflect the then current 'grecian' vogue. Weaknesses in the drawing of the girl and the inconsistent perspective suggest Greuze may have been overreaching himself. The Academy was never to accept him as a history painter.

VIGÉE LE BRUN: *Madame Perregaux* (P457)
It is recorded that the artist was particularly satisfied with this lively portrait of Madame Perregaux (whose husband was banker to the 3rd Marquess of Hertford). The daughter of a portrait painter, the artist married the dealer J.-B.-P. Le Brun in 1776 and - until the fateful year

of 1789, the date of this painting - their Paris *hôtel* was a centre of fashionable society. With the Revolution, she left France to practise with continued success in Italy, Vienna and St Petersburg, returning to Paris only in 1801.

RIESENER: Roll-top Desk (F102)

This superb desk was made by Riesener in 1769 for the *hôtel* (town house) of Pierre Grimod, comte d'Orsay (1748-1809), whose *OR* monogram appears in marquetry on each side. Above the monograms appear the attributes of warfare, perhaps in allusion to Orsay's position as an officer in the dragoons. Other marquetry designs relate to the function of the desk. While closely related in style to the famous *bureau du Roi* (see Gallery 4), F102 is less elaborate in detail, lacking the clock, candelabra and some other gilt-bronze mounts. Riesener was the most versatile cabinet-maker of his time; other pieces by him can be seen in Galleries 3, 13, and, particularly, 24.

Riesener Roll-top Desk (F102)

Boulard Chair (F233)   Houdon *Madame de Sérilly* (S26)

BOULARD: Set of six chairs (F233-8)

Boulard, who worked regularly for the crown from 1777, made these important chairs in 1786 for Louis XVI's card room at Fontainebleau. They formed part of a larger set of thirty-five chairs, eight matching curtains and a screen, all with a blue and white silk *lampas* of the same design as that rewoven for F233-8 in 1982. Chairs with separate cushions, such as these were intended for ladies. Their rather cool, but refined neo-classical design is typical of the taste of the court in its final years before the Revolution. The very fine gilt-bronze **wall-lights** (F374-7) belong to a model made both for Louis XV's daughter, Madame Adélaïde, at Versailles and for Marie-Antoinette at Saint-Cloud; both sets were cast by FELOIX in 1787.

HOUDON: *Madame Victoire de France* (S25) and *Madame de Sérilly* (S26)

The revolution was to have a dramatic effect on the lives of the sculptor and the subjects of these two splendid busts. Madame Victoire (1733-99), the fifth daughter of

Louis XV, was forced to flee France in 1791 with her sister, Madame Adélaïde, and both died as refugees in Italy during the harsh winter of 1799-1800. In 1794, Madame de Sérilly (1763-?99) was accused, with twenty-three others (including her husband and his brother), of having plotted to assist the King. All but Madame de Sérilly were guillotined; she escaped on the unfounded belief that she was pregnant. Houdon, the culminating figure in the evolution of eighteenth-century French portrait sculpture, fell into relative obscurity with the collapse of the *ancien régime*. These works of 1777 (s25) and 1782 (s26) belong to the most successful decades of his career.

Gallery 16
(Formerly the Large Drawing Room)
Sèvres porcelain, Boulle furniture and seventeenth to nineteenth-century landscapes

Sèvres porcelain: Inkstand (C488)

This remarkable inkstand, made in 1758, is one of only three of its design known today. The terrestial globe contained the inkwell, and the celestial globe the sand-shaker

Sèvres porcelain Inkstand (C488)

(for drying ink). The cushion contained a cleaning-sponge, and a bell (now lost) was within the crown. It was almost certainly given by Louis XV to his third daughter, Marie-Adélaïde (1732-1800), whose *MA* monogram appears on one side. However, when the 4th Marquess of Hertford bought the piece in 1843, the monogram was implausibly interpreted as that of Marie-Antoinette (1755-93), who was said to have used the inkstand to write her farewells before being taken to the guillotine.

Sèvres porcelain: Toilet Service (C458-65)

This service, of the finest quality, may well have been intended for Madame de Pompadour as it was left incomplete shortly before her death in 1764. One would expect additional items such as boxes, cups, mirrors, ring stands and candlesticks. She was notoriously vain in her attempts to maintain her beauty. The largest pair of pots were for hair powder of scented starch, airtight seals excluding both dampness and mites; the tall pair were for hair grease; and the smallest pair for the fashionable and suggestive black face patches. There is also a clothes brush and a small *vergette* for dusting wig powder from the shoulders.

Sèvres porcelain: Garniture of three Vases (C334-6)

Garnitures of Sèvres porcelain vases often served as diplomatic gifts (partly to promote French craftsmanship): this garniture with jewelled enamelling was given in this way by Louis XVI to Prince Henry of Prussia in 1784. When acquired in 1860, it was, at 63,000 francs, the 4th Marquess of Hertford's most expensive purchase of Sèvres porcelain.

Gallery 17

(Formerly the Small Drawing Room)

Canaletto and Guardi; Louis XV furniture

CANALETTO: *Two views of the Bacino, Venice* (P497 and P499)

Canaletto, whose work was highly favoured by English patrons, painted this impressive pair of complementary

Rubens *The Adoration of the Magi* (P521)

RUBENS: oil sketches (P519-24)

Rubens was a remarkably prolific artist who produced many oil sketches either in preparation for large-scale paintings or as tapestry designs. *The Defeat and Death of Maxentius* (P520) is an example of the latter, one of a series of twelve scenes illustrating the life of the Roman Emperor Constantine the Great. The two sketches of the *Adoration of the Magi* are *modelli* for well-known altarpieces in Antwerp (P519) and (now) King's College, Cambridge (P521), and were painted in 1624 and 1633 respectively. Most impressive of all in their freshness and vivacity, are the three sketches (P522-4) of 1628 relating to a cycle of paintings glorifying the *Life of Henri IV*. This was commissioned by the subject's widow, Marie de Médicis (whose own life had been celebrated in an earlier series), but abandoned after her exile from France in 1631.

Brouwer *A Boor Asleep* (P211)

BROUWER: *A Boor Asleep* (P211)

In this unpretentious panel can be seen the paradox of
Dutch and Flemish genre painting: low-life subjects painted in a wonderfully delicate manner. In the eighteenth
century such subject matter deterred many English collectors, while the fine handling appealed to their French
counterparts. The 3rd Marquess, who bought P211, and
the 4th Marquess shared this French taste, as can be seen
by the number of fine Dutch cabinet pictures in the
collection. Brouwer lived in Haarlem and later Antwerp;
both Rubens and Rembrandt owned several of his pictures, and his peasant scenes clearly influenced TENIERS,
and A. and I. VAN OSTADE, all represented in this Gallery.

Ascribed to REMBRANDT: *Landscape with a Coach* (P229)

This marvellous panorama seems to encompass the whole range of human experience: rich man and poor, castle and farm, city and landscape, fair skies and foul - all achieved with an almost monochrome palette. The attribution of this picture, one of the 3rd Marquess's most impressive acquisitions, has been much debated; it shares some characteristics of landscapes from the late 1630s by both Rembrandt and his pupil FLINCK. Other pictures once thought to be by Rembrandt, but now regarded as probably by his pupils are: *Rembrandt in a black cap* (P52); *The Good Samaritan* (P203); and *A Boy in fanciful costume* (P201) - all dating from the 1630s.

Gallery 20

(Built with Gallery 21 as a picture gallery, 1872-5)

Dutch seventeenth and eighteenth-century paintings

STEEN: *Celebrating the Birth* (P111)

At first sight the depiction of an innocent family party, this picture, as with the other works by Steen in this room, is a satire on the foolishness of man. The real father

Steen *Celebrating the Birth* (P111)

(perhaps a self-portrait) makes a cuckold's sign over the baby's head, while the official father pays the midwife; a pregnant woman sits drinking to the left. A sterile marriage may be symbolized by the broken eggs, closed jug and bed warmer (providing the only warmth in the marriage bed); and the hanging sausage - like the cuckold gesture, painted out in the nineteenth century - provides further innuendo.

METSU: *The Sleeping Sportsman* (P251)

Metsu, like Steen, was from Leiden, and shared his taste for good-humoured moralising. In P251 we are invited to laugh at the drunken sportsman, whose intemperance has lost him the cockerel - and perhaps the favours of the lady ('to bird' in Dutch slang means to copulate). Other paintings by Metsu in this room, all of a high quality, may be compared with works of a similar character by TER BORCH, NETSCHER and E. VAN DER NEER. In the later seventeenth century, Leiden was famous for its school of 'fine painters', in which the emphasis was on meticulous technique; the paintings of W. VAN MIERIS continued this tradition into the eighteenth century.

DE HOOCH: *A Woman peeling Apples* (P23)

Born in Rotterdam, de Hooch moved to Delft in the early 1650s and, under the influence of Maes and Vermeer, began painting quiet but exquisitely composed domestic scenes in which light is painted with great subtlety. In P23, once attributed to Vermeer, the subject is probably symbolic of domestic virtue.

W. VAN DE VELDE the younger: *Calm: Fishing Boats at low water* (P143)

Willem the younger shared a studio with his father, Willem, and brother, ADRIAEN (whose *Noonday Rest* (P199) hangs in this Gallery). He specialised in marine subjects and, after moving to London with his father in 1672/3, he established the standard for successive generations of English marine artists. P143, dated *c.*1660, is a particularly well-balanced and delicately coloured composition. Several other fine pictures by him hang nearby, while his large and impressive *Calm: Dutch Ships coming to anchor* (P137) is in Gallery 22.

Van de Velde *Calm: Fishing Boats at low water* (P143)

Gallery 21

Dutch seventeenth-century paintings influenced by the landscape and art of Italy

This Gallery is also used for temporary special exhibitions.

J. BOTH: *Italian Landscape* (P28)

Both, who came from Utrecht, was one of the first of his generation of Dutch artists to visit Italy, staying in Rome 1638-42. His paintings and those of earlier Dutch 'Italianate' artists influenced several contemporaries, including BERCHEM, A. CUYP and PYNACKER. This picture, with its carefully constructed composition and glowing colour, is typical of Both's work from the mid-1640s.

A. CUYP: *The Ferry Boat* (P54)

The Ferry Boat, like its companions by Cuyp, *Shipping on the Maas* (P49), and *The Avenue at Meerdervoort* (P51), can be dated to the early 1650s, and is perhaps the finest of the group. All three depict scenes on or near the River Maas beside Cuyp's home town of Dordrecht. Cuyp's paintings

71

Cuyp *The Ferry Boat* (P54)

exerted a particular fascination for British collectors, and even today there are more of his works in this country than any other.

PHILIPS WOUWERMANS: *The Horse Fair* (P65)

In the eighteenth century *The Horse Fair* was celebrated as one of Wouwermans' masterpieces and was engraved when in a French collection. Wouwermans' animated scenes then influenced Watteau and his pupils (see, for example, LANCRET: *Fête in a Wood* (P448) in Gallery 24). The silvery tone of P65, from the 1660s, is even more evident in the slightly earlier *Stream in hilly Country* (P218). *Shoeing a Horse* (P144), of *c*.1650, best displays the earlier influence on him of the Dutch Italianate painters.

BERCHEM: *The Musical Shepherdess* (P640)

Berchem, who was born in Haarlem, probably went to Italy in 1653, although he may have travelled there in 1642-5 with J.B. WEENIX, whose work certainly influenced *A Southern Harbour Scene* (P25). In P640, of 1658, both landscape and figures are painted in an idealized manner, in contrast to the naturalism of Ruisdael, Hobbema or Wijnants. Such Italianate pictures were greatly admired in the eighteenth century, but came to be disparaged (as contrived and unpatriotic) in the later nineteenth century.

Titian *Perseus and Andromeda* (P11)

Gallery 22
(Built as a gallery in 1872-5)
Titian, English portraits, seventeenth century paintings and bronze statuettes

The largest room in Hertford House, Gallery 22 offers one of the finest displays of European painting to be seen anywhere in the world. The seventeenth century is superbly represented by pictures acquired in almost every case, including all those discussed below, by the 4th Marquess of Hertford.

TITIAN: *Perseus and Andromeda* (P11)

Painted for Philip II of Spain in 1554 and later owned by van Dyck, for twenty years *Perseus and Andromeda* was hung by Sir Richard Wallace over a bath at Hertford House (when it was thought to be by Domenichino). It is, in fact, one of Titian's most important works, painted for his greatest patron, and one of a set of six *poesie* (poetical subjects) drawn from the Roman poet Ovid (for another see Gallery 21). It shows Andromeda chained to a rock in sacrifice to a sea monster sent by Neptune, the sea god; her mother had alleged she was more beautiful than Neptune's sea nymphs. Perseus, who chanced upon the scene, plunges down from the sky to slay the monster, watched by Andromeda's parents on the shore. Titian's placement of Andromeda as a full-length nude at one side of the picture, counterbalanced by the smaller but dramatic figure of Perseus, gorgeously clothed, is the kind of mannerist device more usually associated with his compatriot Tintoretto.

DE CHAMPAIGNE: *The Annunciation* (P134)

The archangel Gabriel tells Mary that she will bear a son, Jesus, by the Holy Spirit. The splendour of the figures and their magnificent draperies are emphasized by the bareness of the interior while the remarkable simplicity of the composition may reflect the influence of the Jansenist movement, an austere Catholic sect with which Champaigne was allied. Born in Brussels, he moved to France and became a naturalized Frenchman. It is uncertain for which French church Champaigne painted this altarpiece, but it had been removed before 1815 when it belonged to Napoleon's maternal uncle, Cardinal Fesch. De Champaigne is magnificently represented in Gallery 22. Together with *The Annunciation*, painted probably in the 1640s, can be seen *The Adoration of the Shepherds* (P129), from the same period but very different in its indebtedness to Rubens, *The Marriage of the Virgin* (P119), which may include the artist's self-portrait on the extreme left, and the sympathetic characterization of *An Echevin of Paris* (P127), a fragment cut from a group portrait of officials of the Paris City Council.

ROSA: *Landscape with Apollo and the Cumaean Sibyl* (P116)

The subject is derived from Ovid's *Metamorphoses*. In return for her favours, Apollo offered a prophetess, the Cumaean Sibyl, anything she desired. When she asked for as many years of life as the grains of sand she held in her hands (the scene in Rosa's painting), her wish was granted. But she rebuffed Apollo, and in revenge the god did not give her perpetual youth, so she lived for centuries as a wretched hag. The picture probably dates from the 1650s and was once owned by Cardinal Mazarin. One of Rosa's largest and grandest works, the eerie landscape echoes the tragedy of the story. Rosa was a contemporary of Claude and Gaspard Dughet (see Claude's *Landscape with Apollo and Mercury* (P114) and Dughet's *Falls of Tivoli* (P139) also in Gallery 22), but, unlike them, he drew his inspiration from Italy's mountainous regions or, as here, the rugged coast near Naples, rather than the tranquil views and picturesque sites of the Roman Campagna.

POUSSIN: *A Dance to the Music of Time* (P108)

This grave subject, an allegory typical of its time, was commissioned from Poussin by a learned patron of the fine arts in Rome, Giulio Rospigliosi, later Pope Clement IX. The dancing group represents the perpetual cycle of the human condition: from Poverty (the male figure with the wreath of dried leaves), Labour leads to Riches and thus Pleasure which, indulged to excess, reverts to Poverty. The bubbles and hourglass symbolize the brevity of life, while the figure of Apollo in the sky and the term with the two-headed Janus (an old head looking back and a young head looking forward) refer to the passage of time through the day and through the ages. The picture probably dates from 1635-6 and, for all its beauty, is one of the most serious ever bought by the 4th Marquess of Hertford.

Rembrandt *Titus, the Artist's Son* (P29)

Rubens *The Rainbow Landscape* (P63)

REMBRANDT: *Titus, the Artist's son* (P29)

Titus van Rijn (1641-68), the only child of Rembrandt and his wife Saskia to survive infancy, is shown here at the age of about sixteen, *c.*1657, shortly after his father had been declared bankrupt. There is a remarkable tenderness in the way Rembrandt looks at his son which is in complete contrast to the formality of the earlier Rembrandt studio portraits commissioned by the Pellicornes (P82 and P90, also in Gallery 22), a merchant family, proud of their success.

RUBENS: *The Rainbow Landscape* (P63)

The Rainbow Landscape was painted by Rubens after he had retired to the château of Het Steen, between Brussels and Antwerp, in 1635. The château itself is the subject of the companion landscape in the National Gallery, London. Together, the pictures offer a glorious celebration of life in the Brabant countryside. Painted probably for the artist's own pleasure, the pictures show contrasting aspects of a summer's day, a morning scene in the National Gallery painting and late afternoon in *The Rainbow Landscape*. When bought at auction for a record price by the 4th Marquess of Hertford in 1856 his competitors included the National Gallery.

Velázquez *The Lady with a Fan* (P88)

Gallery 23

(Built as a gallery in 1872-5)

Nineteenth-century French paintings and miniatures

Paintings are hung close together in an approximation of the manner favoured in that century.

SCHEFFER: *Francesca da Rimini* (P316)

One of the most popular French paintings of the century (George Eliot said that she 'could look at it for hours'), *Francesca da Rimini* cost the 4th Marquess of Hertford more than any other of his nineteenth-century pictures. He bought it at auction in 1870, but it had originally been exhibited at the Salon of 1835. The subject, derived from Dante's *Inferno*, shows Dante, guided by Virgil, watching Paolo and Francesca in the second circle of Hell with the souls of the lustful. The lovers had been stabbed to death by Francesca's husband, who was also Paolo's elder brother. The ornate frame, which includes part of Dante's text, elaborates the story and was made for the painting when it was in the collection of the Russian collector Anatole Demidoff (1812-70).

Scheffer *Francesca da Rimini* (P316)

VERNET: *The Dog of the Regiment Wounded* (P607)

The 4th Marquess of Hertford was an enthusiastic collector of works of art and books relating to Napoleon's military exploits, due, presumably, to his upbringing in Paris during the Empire and his later friendship with Napoleon III. Horace Vernet was also a devotee of the Napoleonic legend, painting portraits of the Emperor, episodes from his life and scenes from the lives of his soldiers on and off the battlefield. Painted in 1819, *The Dog of the Regiment Wounded*, together with its pendant *The Wounded Trumpeter* (P613), were immensely popular pictures, as one might expect from their combination of sentimentality with military glamour. In 1863 the critic Sainte-Beuve remembered engravings of them 'in every shop window'.

ROQUEPLAN: *The Lion in Love* (P285)

The subject is taken from La Fontaine's *Fables*. A noble lion fell in love with a shepherdess. Her father insisted that the lion must have his claws and teeth removed, whereupon the dogs were set on him. The picture was a considerable success at the 1836 Salon and was bought by the 4th Marquess of Hertford in 1853. Scenes from history and literature were a staple part of nineteenth-century painting, particularly for those of Lord Hertford's generation whose formative years coincided with the full flood of romanticism in the 1820s and 1830s. Within that movement, however, his taste tended towards a restrained sentimentality rather than passionate intensity.

MEISSONIER: *An Artist showing his Work* (P325)

The vogue among painters like Roqueplan, Isabey and Meissonier for subject matter derived from the eighteenth century was part of a general revival of interest in the *ancien régime* which with painting had begun by the 1840s. The revival entirely agreed with the tastes of the 4th Marquess of Hertford. Meissonier's figures in this picture (which was exhibited at the Salon of 1850-1) wear Louis XV costumes but he has shown his own pictures on the studio walls. Meissonier was perhaps the most successful French painter of the nineteenth century, both financially and in terms of the official honours that were conferred upon him. The 4th Marquess had a particular fondness for his anecdotal, highly finished art and they knew each other well.

Isabey *Self-Portrait* (M226)

In the centre of the gallery is a case containing early nineteenth-century miniatures (please lift the covers). Many relate to the Emperor Napoleon and his family. Included are fine examples by Isabey and Augustin, who were perhaps the leading French miniature painters of the early years of the nineteenth century.

ISABEY: *Self-portrait* (M226)

Isabey and his studio produced hundreds of miniatures, particularly of Napoleon and his court. After 1815 he worked with equal facility for the victorious allied powers (note the *Portrait of Wellington* (M223)) and for the Bourbon monarchy. His considerable abilities can perhaps be best seen in his early work such as this *Self-Portrait*, painted on ivory *c.*1800.

Gallery 24

(Formerly the dressing-rooms of Sir Richard and Lady Wallace and Lady Wallace's bathroom)

Eighteenth-century French furniture and paintings, also miniatures

Attributed to GAUDREAUS: Chest of Drawers (F85)

Once thought to be by Cressent, this chest of drawers is now attributed to Gaudreaus by analogy with a chest of drawers delivered by Gaudreaus in 1744 to Louis XV's château at Choisy. F85 was probably made for Monsieur de Selle, a wealthy holder of a sinecure in the naval department. Now believed to date from *c.*1735-40, it is particularly notable for its superb dragon mounts and *espagnolette* head. The marquetry is of kingwood in an oyster-work pattern, and the marble top is original.

OEBEN: Combined Toilet- and Writing-Table (F110)

From the middle of the eighteenth century pieces of furniture combining two or more functions were frequently produced. The workshop of Oeben in which this table was made, perhaps by Leleu (the piece carries an incised mark with his name), was noted for its production of elaborate fitments and complicated locking devices, as fitted to the great roll-top desk in Gallery 15. This ingeniously designed table contains four drawers, a stamped leather writing surface and a toilet mirror. The fittings are controlled by a complex lock which allows them to be opened out in accordance with the intended use of the table.

RIESENER: Drop-front Secretaire (F300)

This is perhaps the most imposing of the four splendid drop-front desks (or secretaires) displayed in Gallery 24. It was made in 1780 by Jean-Henri Riesener, the leading cabinet-maker of the period, for Queen Marie-Antoinette's apartments at Versailles and was used by the Queen herself. The interior contains pigeon-holes and drawers for papers and writing materials. Indeed, the secretaires differ in purpose from the chests of drawers in this gallery in being functional pieces rather than ornamental furniture within a decorative scheme. The ornate marquetry of purple-, tulip- and other woods is more typical of furniture of the 1760s and is indicative of the slowness with which the court adapted to changes in taste at this time.

Riesener Drop-front Secretaire (F302)

RIESENER: Drop-front Secretaire (F302)

Like F300, this secretaire was made by Riesener for Marie-Antoinette, although for the Petit Trianon at Versailles rather than her apartments in the palace. The smaller size of the rooms at the Petit Trianon probably accounts for its narrow width. Delivered in 1783, it is in a more advanced taste than F300, particularly in its use of finely chased, naturalistic mounts. The lozenge-shaped marquetry (in *satiné* and holly) with a motif of water-lilies (in sycamore) is a feature of Riesener's work. The similar **secretaire** in Gallery 24 (F303) veneered with thuya-wood bordered with purplewood, was also made by Riesener for Marie-Antoinette at Versailles and is displayed with a **corner cupboard** (F275) made *en suite*.

WATTEAU: *The Music Party* (P410)

The 4th Marquess of Hertford was an enthusiastic admirer of the pictures of Watteau and his pupils Lancret and Pater. Their elegance had a particular appeal for the rich collectors of the Second Empire after a period of comparative neglect during and after the Revolution. *The Music Party*, painted *c*.1718, is the most elaborate of several pictures with the theme of a standing musician playing before a small group of elegantly dressed listeners. The mood of chivalrous dalliance among the figures, hinted rather than expressed, is a characteristic feature of Watteau's subtle scenes, as is the ambiguous stage-like setting.

WATTEAU: *Gilles and his Family* (P381)

The theatre had a great influence on Watteau's subject matter as well as the structure of his compositions. The figures in *Gilles and his Family* and in *Harlequin and Columbine* (P387) wear the costume of characters in the Italian *commedia dell'arte*, although we know from a drawing that the guitarist dressed as Gilles or Mezzetin is Watteau's friend Pierre Sirois, a dealer in glass. It is perhaps in paintings on a small scale that Watteau came closest to the matchless delicacy of his drawings.

Watteau *Gilles and his Family*
(P381)

FRAGONARD: *The Swing* (P430)

Before painting this picture in 1767, Fragonard was
thought to be destined for a great career as a history
painter, the most esteemed calling for an eighteenth-
century artist. But after receiving the commission for this
work from an unknown patron, he turned increasingly to
genre scenes, portraits and landscapes, usually in a high-
spirited decorative manner. The range of his art is well
shown in Gallery 24, from his early *Musical Contest* (P471),
very much in the style of his master Boucher, to the more
sombre and sculptural *Fountain of Love* (P394) of the 1780s.
The exuberance of *The Swing* has come to epitomize
painting under the *ancien régime*, but with little historical
accuracy. The fact that the history painters (except David)
have been largely forgotten, and were to be of no interest
to nineteenth-century collectors like the 4th Marquess of
Hertford, would have astonished most observers of
Fragonard's own generation.

Fragonard *The Swing* (P430)

Boizot, Gouthière and Delunésy The Avignon Clock (F258)

Horenbout *Portrait of Holbein* (M205)

In the centre of the gallery are two covered hexagonal cases containing English and Continental miniatures from the sixteenth to the end of the eighteenth centuries (please lift the covers). Both portraits and subject paintings (mostly scenes of gallantry) are well represented.

HORENBOUT: *Portrait of Holbein* (M203)

For long thought to be a self-portrait by Holbein, the style of this miniature (case 2) is now believed to be closer to the work of Lucas Horenbout, who taught Holbein the techniques of miniature painting. Painted on vellum in 1543, the year of Holbein's death, it may well be a memorial portrait.

HALL: *The Painter's Family* (M186)

The Swedish-born Hall established himself as the leading portrait miniaturist soon after he settled in Paris in 1766. This work (case 1), painted on ivory in the mid 1770s, shows him at the height of his powers.

Gallery 25

(Formerly Lady Wallace's bedroom)

Eighteenth-century French furniture and paintings

BOIZOT, GOUTHIÈRE and DELUNÉSY: The Avignon Clock (F258)

Designed by the sculptor Boizot and chased and gilt by Gouthière, this mantel clock, with a movement by Delunésy, was presented by the city of Avignon to the marquis de Rochechouart in 1771. In 1768 Rochechouart had taken back Avignon from papal control on behalf of Louis XV and had become its governor. The figure representing the city holds a wreath over the Rochechouart coat of arms, while the reclining male figure represents the River Rhône and the seated female its tributary, the Durance.

GOUTHIÈRE: Perfume Burner (F292)

The tripod of this perfume burner, with its bowl of red jasper, is one of the finest works of Pierre Gouthière, the leading maker of gilt bronzes before the Revolution.

Later eighteenth-century bronzes are notably more delicate than those produced earlier in the century. The perfume burner was made in the 1770s for the duc d'Aumont (who after the death of Louis XV also owned the great chest of drawers F86 in Gallery 4) and was acquired at his sale in 1782 by Marie-Antoinette.

DUBOIS: Chest of Drawers (F245)

This chest of drawers was once thought to have been the marriage coffer of Marie-Antoinette. Made in the 1760s, it combines neo-classical and Oriental elements, a slightly eccentric combination but one frequently found in furniture of this period. The gilt-bronze caryatids are in the style of the sculptor Falconet and the oval plaque is of Japanese lacquer combined with a fretted mount of pseudo-Oriental character.

BOUCHER: *Jupiter and Callisto* (P446)

Boucher's art contains numerous erotic mythological subjects. The four rectangular canvases with scenes in which Venus plays a prominent part (P429, P432, P438 and P444) were not originally a set, but by 1851 they had been mounted together on a folding screen. The large oval *Jupiter and Callisto*, dated 1769, is one of Boucher's last works and shows the blander handling and colour of his final years. Jupiter, disguised as Diana, seduces Callisto, one of Diana's hunting nymphs.

BOUCHER: *Madame de Pompadour* (P418)

Jeanne-Antoinette Poisson (1721-64) became the mistress of Louis XV and was created marquise de Pompadour in 1745. A lavish supporter of the arts, she took a close interest both in the sumptuous furnishing of her town houses and châteaux and in the fortunes and products of the Sèvres porcelain factory. From Boucher she commissioned portraits, and mythological and religious works. Indeed, of the twelve known portraits by Boucher, seven are of Madame de Pompadour. This example, signed and dated 1759, shows her standing beside a sculpture portraying Friendship consoling Love, very close in design to a work which she had commissioned from Pigalle to symbolize her later, platonic relationship with the king.

Boucher *Madame de Pompadour* (P418)

Wallace Collection Publications

Catalogues

Pictures I British, German, Italian, Spanish, by John Ingamells, 1985

Pictures II French Nineteenth Century, by John Ingamells, 1986

Pictures III French before 1815, by John Ingamells, 1989

Pictures IV Dutch and Flemish, by John Ingamells, 1992

Summary Illustrated Catalogue of Pictures, by John Ingamells, 1979

Miniatures, by Graham Reynolds, 1980

Illuminated Manuscript Cuttings, by J.J.G. Alexander, 1980

Sculpture, by [Sir] James Mann, 1931, with Supplement, 1982

Furniture, 3 vols., by Peter Hughes, 1996

Pottery, Maiolica, Faience, Stoneware, by A.V.B. Norman, 1976

Sèvres Porcelain, 3 vols., by Rosalind Savill, 1988

European Arms and Armour, 2 vols., by Sir James Mann, 1962

European Arms and Armour Supplement, by A.V.B. Norman, 1986

Oriental Arms and Armour, by Guy Francis Laking, 1913, with Supplement, 1964

Guides and Booklets

Guide to the Armouries, 1982

The Hertford Mawson Letters, by John Ingamells, 1981

The Wallace Collection, by John Ingamells, 1990

The Founders of the Wallace Collection, by Peter Hughes, 1992

Monographs

Mrs Robinson and her Portraits, by John Ingamells, 1978

Richard Parkes Bonington, by John Ingamells, 1979

Eighteenth-Century France and the East, by Peter Hughes, 1981

Rembrandt 1892, by John Ingamells, 1992